by **Molly Bang**
& **Penny Chisholm**
illustrated by **MOLLY BANG**

THE BLUE SKY PRESS
An Imprint of Scholastic Inc.
New York

BURIED SUNLIGHT

HOW FOSSIL FUELS HAVE CHANGED THE EARTH

I AM YOUR SUN, YOUR GOLDEN STAR.

Even from 93 million miles away,

I warm your land, your seas, your air,

and chase the darkness from your days.

My energy gives light and life

to your tiny Earth.

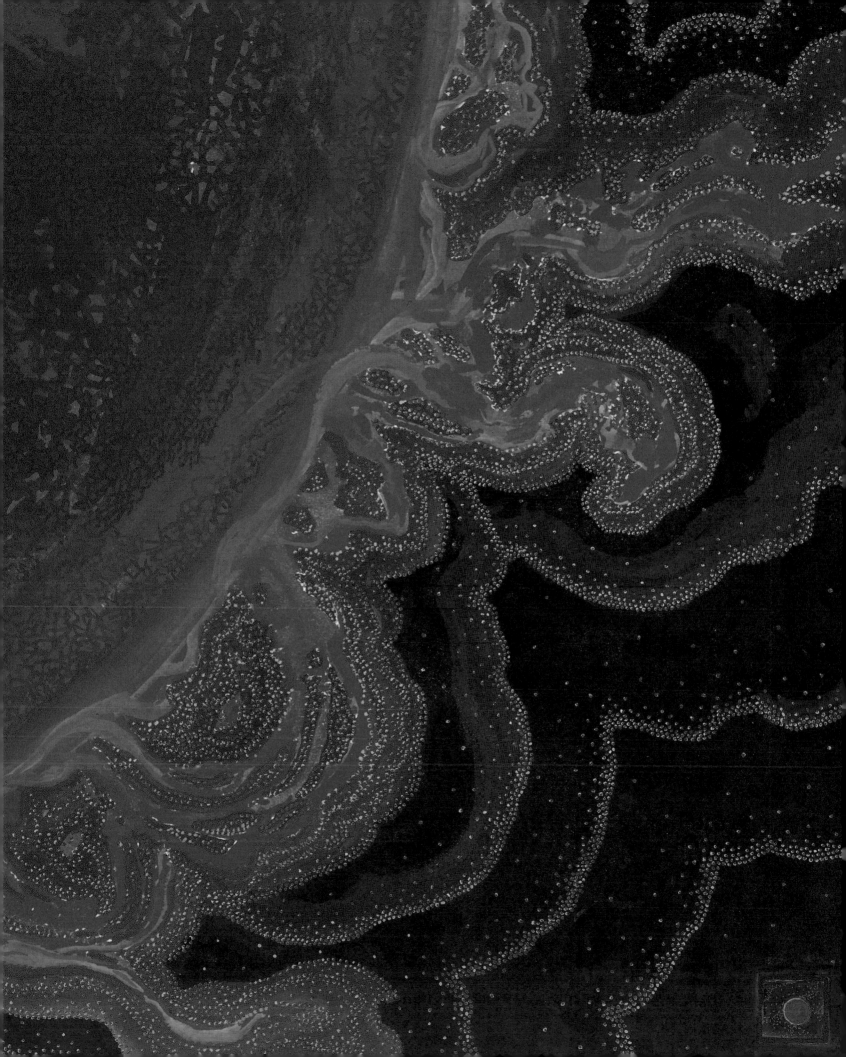

Yes, living things—including YOU—
need energy to stay alive and grow.

But you also use energy to heat
your houses, to cook your food,

to move your cars and trains and ocean ships,
to run your computers and machines.

Where does that energy come from?

Most of it
comes from coal
and oil and gas,
called fossil fuels.

What makes them
"FOSSILS"?

Like dinosaurs, they
are ancient life that was
buried deep underground.
But fossil fuels are ancient
PLANTS. They captured
light I shined on Earth
millions of years ago.

All this time, those fossil
plants have kept my
sunlight-energy locked
inside themselves.

GAS

OIL

COAL

When you burn fossil fuels, you free the energy locked inside those ancient plants and turn it into heat and light.

But how did those plants catch my sunlight-energy and lock it into themselves?

BURNING COAL

PHOTOSYNTHESIS!

O$_2$

CO$_2$

CARBON CHAINS

This is what happens:
Green plants everywhere
catch my light and use it to
pull in carbon dioxide (CO_2) from
the air. They use my sunlight-energy
to build chains of carbon—sugar!—
that form their leaves and stems and fruit.
And as they photosynthesize, these
same green plants release oxygen (O_2)
into the air—the air you breathe.

CO_2

O_2

PHYTOPLANKTON

WHAT
HAPPENS
THEN?

YOU gobble up
the plants!
You eat their
carbon
chains!

You breathe in the oxygen
the plants breathed out.
You use it to break the chains
and take their energy, so YOU
can move and live and grow.

CO_2

You breathe out the
broken pieces of the chains
as carbon dioxide, CO_2.

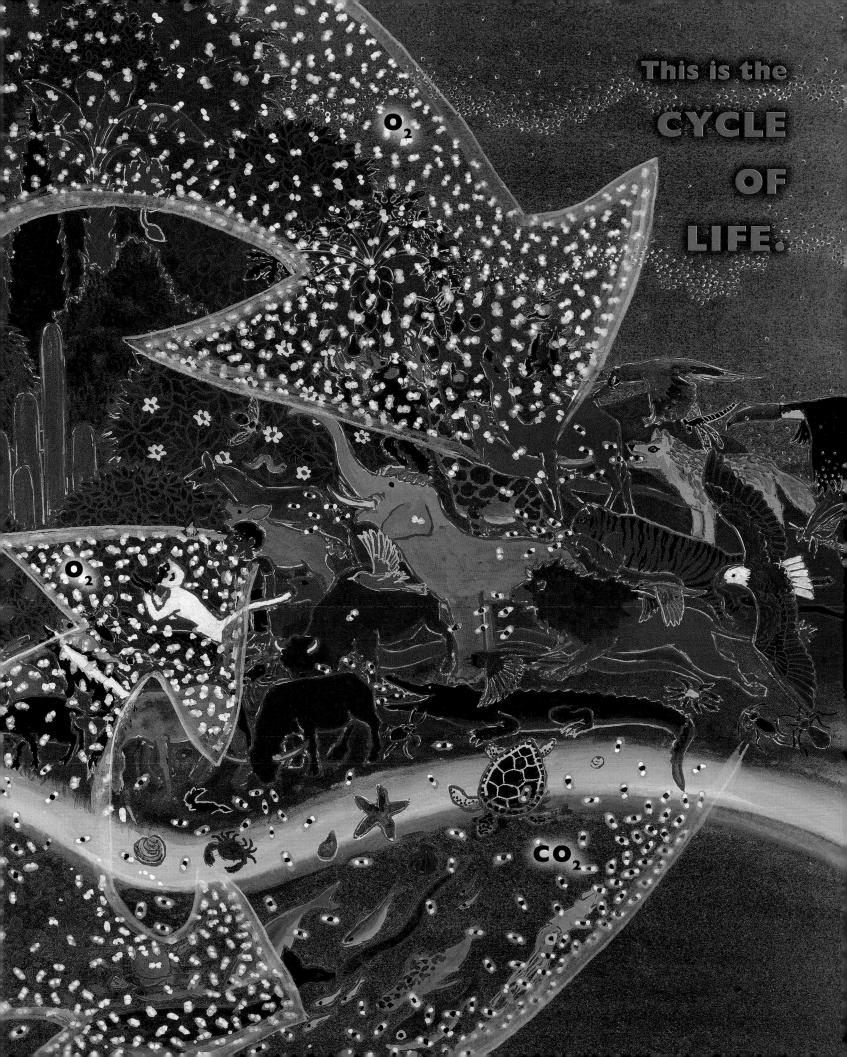

This Cycle of Life is *almost* in perfect balance.

All the plants together make a *tiny* bit more carbon chains than all the animals and bacteria eat.

And the plants breathe out a *tiny* bit more oxygen than the animals and bacteria breathe in.

The difference isn't much, but over MILLIONS AND MILLIONS OF YEARS, a tiny bit each year can make a HUGE difference!

In fact, these tiny differences gave you two of Earth's great treasures: all the oxygen you breathe and fossil fuels.

Here's what happened.

CO_2

Billions of years ago, long before dinosaurs roamed the Earth, there was no life on land.

THERE WAS NO OXYGEN IN THE AIR.
NONE.

Back then, the only life on Earth was tiny bacteria floating in the seas and tiny sea animals that ate them. Eventually, some of those tiny bacteria evolved into tiny green plants!

O_2

CO_2

They caught my light, made carbon-sugar chains, and breathed oxygen out into the sea. Each year, they sent out a little more oxygen than the tiny animals could breathe in.

O_2

So over
MILLIONS AND MILLIONS OF YEARS,
the extra oxygen bubbled into the water
and up . . . until the water and air
were rich with oxygen.

Each year, the tiny plants made
a few more carbon chains than
the tiny sea animals could eat.

So over MILLIONS AND MILLIONS OF
YEARS, the extra carbon chains
piled up on the ocean floor.

Over **MILLIONS AND MILLIONS MORE YEARS,** bigger animals and plants evolved and moved onto land. And like the tiny plants in the sea, the land plants made more carbon chains than the animals and bacteria on land could eat. Each year, those uneaten carbon chains—dead plants—piled up. As even more **MILLIONS AND MILLIONS OF YEARS** passed, all those dead plants (with my energy locked inside) were buried under layers of dirt, on the land and on the bottom of the sea.

CO_2

GAS

OIL

Buried deeper and deeper, they were SQUASHED

and changed into . . .

oil and coal and gas:

O$_2$

COAL

FOSSIL FUELS—
my ancient
buried sunlight.

Those fossil fuels lay deep in the Earth for millions
of years, as new and different creatures evolved.

150 MILLION YEARS AGO

60 MILLION YEARS AGO

Some plants and animals became extinct, and more new
ones evolved, but the Cycle of Life kept circling around.

Eventually—just a few hundred thousand years ago—

15 THOUSAND YEARS AGO

60 MILLION YEARS AGO

150 MILLION YEARS AGO

you humans evolved and spread across the Earth.

You built fires to warm yourselves and cook your food.

And one day, you discovered . . .

CO$_2$

BURNING
COAL

Fossil fuels!

My BURIED

SUNLIGHT!!!

Very quickly, you began
to burn those fossil
fuels—the coal and
oil and gas that took
millions and millions
of years for the Cycle
of Life to make.

GAS

OIL

CO₂

COAL

Now you use my ancient
sunlight-energy to power your world.

When you burn the fossil fuels,
you break their carbon chains,
pull oxygen from the air, and
send out carbon dioxide, CO₂.

Every year, as more fossil fuels are burned,
more CO_2 rises into Earth's air.
Trees and plants and ocean waters pull in
as much as they can, but it's not enough
to keep CO_2 from piling up in the sky.

Your scientists are measuring it.

CO$_2$

They see CO$_2$ is increasing, faster and faster.
And you humans are also cutting
down forests and burning
them to clear the land for growing
food, putting even more CO$_2$ in the air.

"SO WHAT?" some people say.

SO THIS: CO_2 is part of a "blanket" of gases around Earth.
My sunlight passes through the blanket and heats Earth,
but much of the heat bounces back into space.
Certain gases, like CO_2, trap the heat and hold it.
This helps control Earth's temperature.

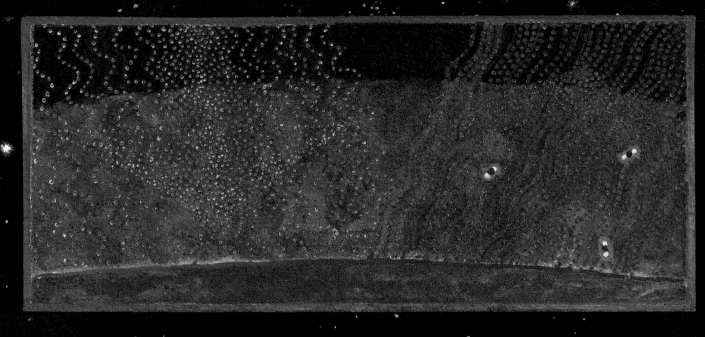

When these gases are lost from the blanket, Earth cools.

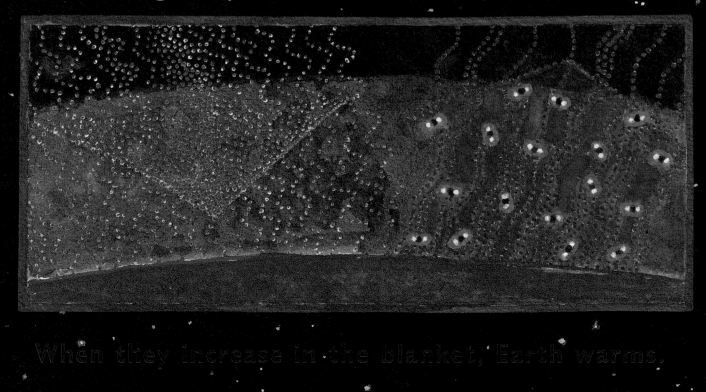

When they increase in the blanket, Earth warms.

**Burning fossil fuels and burning your forests
puts more CO$_2$ into Earth's blanket every year.
It traps more heat and warms the land and seas.**

Your Earth has begun
to feel these changes:
Some Arctic ice and
glaciers are melting.

The seas are warming,
and some are beginning
to creep over the land.

The warming causes
fiercer storms, and
droughts, and floods.

All around the Earth,
weather is slightly
different than it was
in the recent past.

In the future the
changes will likely be
more severe. . . .

Some people still ask, "SO WHAT?"
Earth has changed a LOT over the billions of years
since it was born! It's been MUCH warmer,
and MUCH colder, than it is today!
"Why NOT burn fossil fuels?"

Those people are PARTLY right.

I, your sun, have watched your planet
warm and cool many times.

Earth has been so cold that ice covered
beaches where you go swimming today.
Earth has been so warm that palm trees
once grew where snow falls now.

Cold and warm, cold and warm, your planet goes
through these changes, and it always will.

**EVEN WITHOUT
HUMANS.**

But those changes happened VERY VERY slowly—
over hundreds of thousands of years. The Earth's
living creatures had time to adjust to the changing
climate. But burning fossil fuels has poured huge
quantities of CO_2 into the air in just a few
HUNDRED years.

CO_2

400,000 YEARS AGO

300,000 YEARS AGO

This is VERY VERY VERY VERY fast.

How many living creatures
will be able to adjust
to such rapid changes?
How will it change the
way you humans live?

200,000 YEARS AGO

100,000 YEARS AGO

NOW

Billions of tons of fossil fuels—my sunlight-energy—

still lie locked deep inside the vaults of Earth.

If you burn them up, Earth's CO_2

blanket will grow thicker and thicker.

Your Earth will warm so much it will change

in ways that no one can predict for sure.

But it will change.

Will you humans keep burning

more and more fossil fuels every year

and risk the changes this will bring?

Or will you work together

to use my ancient sunlight more slowly,

find other sources of energy, and invent ways

to thin the blanket of CO_2?

The choice is yours.

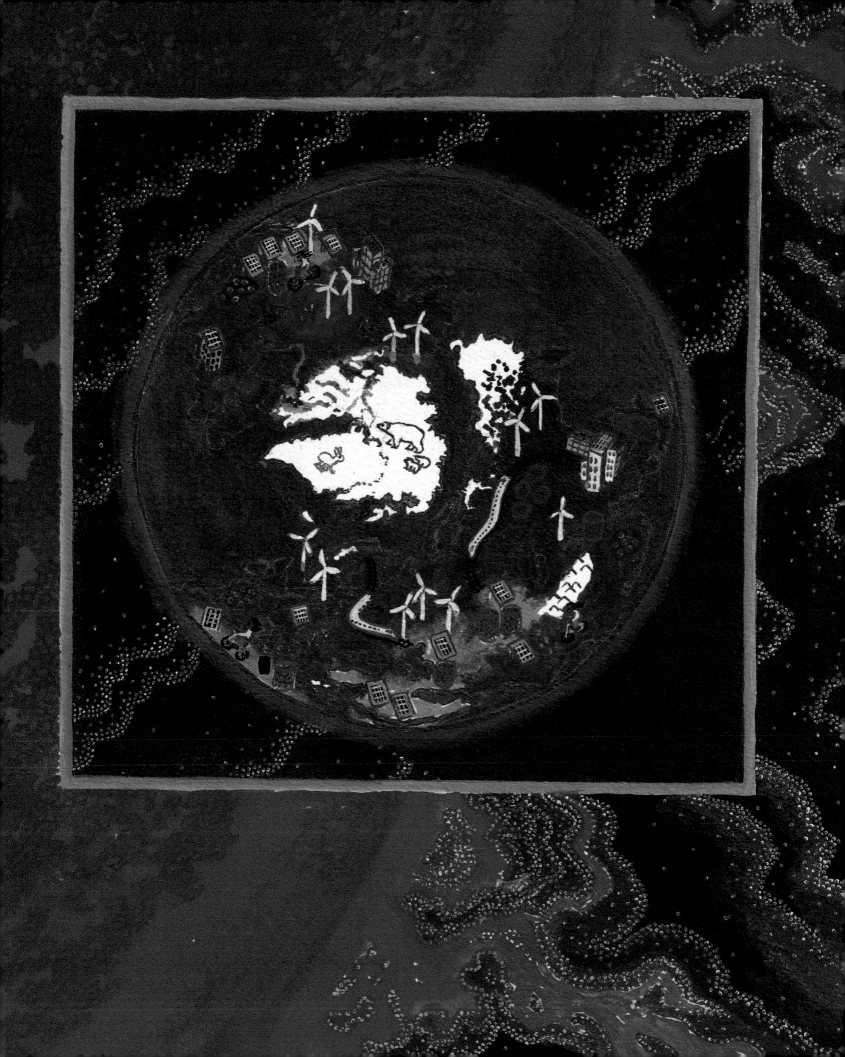

NOTES ABOUT THIS BOOK

SINCE THE 19TH CENTURY, HUMAN CIVILIZATION HAS BEEN RUN ON ANCIENT SUNLIGHT STORED IN FOSSIL FUELS.

This is a book about fossil fuels: where they came from and how using them has changed our species and our planet. Fossil fuel energy is sunlight energy captured by plants and phytoplankton and buried millions of years ago. The use of this ancient sunlight has shaped our modern world.

When we humans started using fossil fuels, we did not understand that our actions could influence the entire planet. Now we know that they can have a profound impact on our Earth and its biosphere. We must consider carefully the impact our choices have on our current world as well as on future generations.

FOSSIL FUELS COME FROM A NATURAL GLOBAL IMBALANCE BETWEEN PHOTOSYNTHESIS AND RESPIRATION.

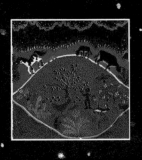

Nearly all life on Earth depends on plants for food: Animals, reptiles, insects, and microorganisms either eat plants or eat other organisms that have eaten plants. Plants make their own food through photosynthesis—using the sun's energy to link carbon atoms from carbon dioxide in the air into chains of sugar, simultaneously releasing oxygen.

CARBON DIOXIDE GAS (CO_2) + WATER (H_2O)
+ SOLAR ENERGY (PHOTONS)
react and make . . .
SUGAR ($C_6H_{12}O_6$) + OXYGEN GAS (O_2)

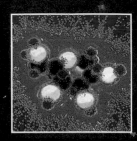

Through photosynthesis, solar energy "comes alive" as the chemical bonds in sugar. To use that captured energy for themselves, animals "burn" the sugar during respiration—the reverse of photosynthesis. Oxygen is consumed, sugar is broken down, and carbon is released as CO_2:

SUGAR ($C_6H_{12}O_6$) + OXYGEN GAS (O_2)
react and make . . .
CARBON DIOXIDE GAS (CO_2) + WATER (H_2O)
+ RELEASED ENERGY FOR BIOLOGICAL WORK

This is what we call the "Cycle of Life": Carbon and oxygen are constantly recycled while energy flows from the sun into chemical bonds that hold the sun's energy. When we and other animals

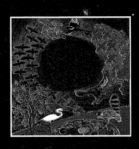

eat, our bodies break the bonds, using oxygen, and take their energy to do the "biological work" that keeps us alive. Each year as they photosynthesize, all of Earth's plants and trees, seaweeds and phytoplankton draw about 60 billion tons of carbon from the air, as CO_2, and build it into living "biomass," or living "organic carbon." This is what feeds life on land and in the sea.

If the global Cycle of Life were always in perfect balance, all the animals and bacteria would use all the oxygen that plants produce to burn all of the carbon chains that those same plants produce.

But the cycle isn't in *perfect* balance.

Usually, there is a *tiny* bit more photosynthesis than respiration globally. This means that a *tiny* bit more organic carbon and a *tiny* bit more oxygen are

produced than are consumed. On *human* time scales—say hundreds of years—these differences are negligible. Today, for example, there is only about 0.2 percent more photosynthesis than respiration. But over millions of years—i.e., *geologic* time scales—these tiny imbalances can accumulate and change the planet. In fact, they created the oxygen in our atmosphere that allowed the evolution of all complex life, including us. AND they created the fossil fuels that made possible extraordinary human progress over the past two hundred years.

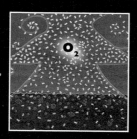

IT TOOK BILLIONS OF YEARS FOR LIFE ON EARTH TO FILL THE AIR WITH OXYGEN, AND MILLIONS OF YEARS TO MAKE FOSSIL FUELS.

Over the last 4.5 billion years, Earth has changed from a fiery ball of molten rock into our living home. At the beginning of Earth's existence, there was no life anywhere and no oxygen in the air. Then, around 3.8 billion years ago, primitive bacteria appeared in the oceans, and eventually some descendants of those bacteria began to photosynthesize, pouring oxygen into the seas and ultimately into the air. Larger algae and plants evolved and, over millions and millions of years, they flooded the air with oxygen. The oxygen-rich oceans and atmosphere shaped Earth and its diversity of life.

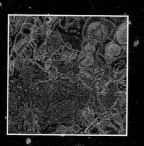

The buildup of oxygen could only have happened if there was more photosynthesis than respiration over vast stretches of time. Why didn't that plant matter get eaten? Because it became buried under layers of mud and rock and sand. And in some places the carbon chains were slowly cooked by heat and pressure, and converted to oil, coal, and gas. These are the sunlight savings bank of our Earth: fossil fuels.

Humans like us first appeared in Africa about 160,000 years ago. By the end of the last ice age 11,000 years ago, we had spread across the planet. For those early humans, the only energy available for food, shelter, and fire was the energy that the sun could provide over a typical human life-span—energy stored in materials such as wood. But when we discovered fossil fuels, we began to use this ancient stored sunlight to power our lives. Fossil fuels also ran our farm machinery and allowed us to make fertilizers, greatly increasing our ability to produce food. Our populations grew and grew, consuming more and more fossil fuels with each generation.

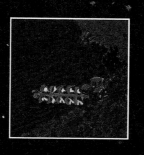

BURNING FOSSIL FUELS HAS NOT ONLY CHANGED OUR LIVES, BUT IT HAS ALSO CHANGED OUR ATMOSPHERE.

It took *hundreds of millions* of years for the Cycle of Life to accumulate and bury Earth's fossil fuels. We've been digging them up and burning them for just *hundreds* of years. In other words, we have been using the sunlight energy in Earth's savings bank about a million times faster than the Earth is able to catch and store new sunlight. And as we burn fossil fuels—breaking their carbon bonds to extract energy—we are pouring

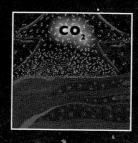

carbon dioxide into the atmosphere. Each year, the burning of fossil fuels—and vast forested regions—releases roughly 9 billion tons of carbon, as CO_2, into the air. Ocean waters and plants and trees on land take up about half of that extra CO_2; the other half is piling up in the atmosphere.

In just a few hundred years, our human activities have caused a 40 percent increase in atmospheric CO_2. That is *faster* than the Earth's atmosphere has ever changed before. And there are still trillions of tons of fossil fuels buried deep in the Earth. If we dig them all up and burn them, and continue to burn our forests, the carbon dioxide concentration in our atmosphere could be *4–5 times* what it is today.

WHY SHOULD WE BE CONCERNED ABOUT RISING CO_2 IN THE ATMOSPHERE?

The temperature of Earth depends on the amount of sunlight it receives, how much of that is reflected back into space, and the kinds and amounts of heat-trapping gases in its atmosphere. Those heat-trapping gases, called "greenhouse" gases, let sunlight through,

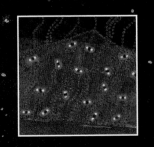

but they trap its heat in their chemical bonds as it bounces off the Earth and radiates back toward space. The heat-trapping gases form a "thermal blanket" around the Earth. Without that blanket, Earth's *average* temperature would be 0°Fahrenheit. In contrast, if our atmosphere had as much CO_2 as Venus, our Earth would be too hot for life. The temperature of Venus is 867°F!

Other important greenhouse gases are water vapor (H_2O), methane (CH_4), nitrous oxide (N_2O), and ozone (O_3). Like carbon dioxide, atmospheric methane and nitrous oxide have been steadily increasing since the beginning of the industrial era. Molecule for molecule they are much stronger greenhouse gases than CO_2, so as they continue to increase they will become more important in greenhouse warming.

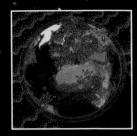

IF WE CONTINUE TO BURN FOSSIL FUELS, WHAT WILL THAT MEAN FOR OUR LIVES?

Since we began to burn fossil fuels and vast forests, the CO_2 in our atmosphere has increased by 40 percent, and average temperatures around the world have increased 1.4°F. Arctic temperatures have increased by twice this global average, and there has been a dramatic

decrease in the sea ice of the Arctic Ocean. It will soon be ice free. We cannot be sure that *all* of this warming is due to increased greenhouse gases, but mounting evidence indicates they play a significant role.

Scientists predict that if we continue to burn fossil fuels, Earth's average surface temperatures will likely rise 4–10°F by the end of the century. We can expect more melting glaciers and ice caps, and sea levels rising by as much as three feet. Climate in general will change; droughts and floods will be more severe and storms more violent. As the oceans absorb much of the extra CO_2, they will become more acid, dissolving corals and animals with shells such as

clams and oysters. Eventually, whole ecosystems will change with shifts in the types of plants and animals that can live in them.

GEOLOGISTS KNOW THE EARTH CHANGED A LOT IN THE PAST BEFORE HUMANS EVEN EXISTED. HOW IS THIS DIFFERENT?

Indeed, throughout its 4.5 billion years, our Earth has been an ever-changing planet. After life appeared, it evolved with these changes. Recently, over the last 800,000 years, our planet has experienced regularly occurring ice ages with warm periods in between. Multiple factors cause these types of changes, including volcanic activity, the shifting of continents, and differences in the Earth's tilt and orbit around

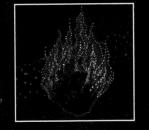

the sun. The response of the biosphere to these changes also plays a role, and all these factors influence climate *and* each other, so understanding the causes of past climate cycles is a huge challenge.

Scientists have measured CO_2 concentrations frozen in ancient ice to help us understand the relationship between atmospheric CO_2 and past climate change, as well as how much the CO_2 concentration has changed since humans began burning fossil fuels. Despite the complexities and uncertainties, we do know this: 1) the levels of CO_2 in the atmosphere have been increasing steadily over the past one hundred years due to burning fossil fuels and deforestation; 2) CO_2 is a

"heat-trapping" gas; and 3) the Earth is warming. Given this knowledge, we have a choice: Do we continue to use fossil fuels at current rates and risk the consequences of a quickly warming planet? Or do we move as soon as possible to alternative forms of energy and conservation?

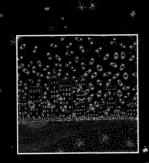

SO WHAT WILL WE USE FOR ENERGY AS WE SHIFT AWAY FROM FOSSIL FUELS?

No single energy source can replace fossil fuels. While there are many different technologies and approaches to collecting, storing, and distributing alternative energy sources, the fundamental non-fossil energy sources available to us are the following:

SOLAR ENERGY:

We can collect the sun's energy directly through absorption into solar hot-water panels or by photovoltaic cells. We can also collect it in fast-growing plants such as corn, grass, and sugar cane—and microscopic algae—because they all photosynthesize and lock solar energy into their biomass as they grow. This

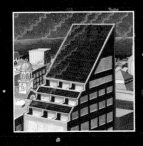

"biomass energy" is like fossil fuel energy, but it doesn't take millions of years to generate. It is created and used in a short period of time, and thus it is renewable. It does not add any more CO_2 to the atmosphere than it draws out.

ENERGY FROM GRAVITY:

The ocean's tides are caused by gravitational forces between the Earth and the moon, and the energy in tides can be captured for our use.

ENERGY FROM GRAVITY COMBINED WITH SOLAR:
Gravity and the sun drive the global water cycle—evaporation, clouds, rain, and river flow— which can be captured as hydroelectric power. They also create the wind, which can be captured with wind turbines.

GEOTHERMAL ENERGY FROM THE EARTH'S INTERIOR:
The interior of the Earth is very hot. In certain places, that heat is carried near the surface of the Earth and can be captured and converted into heat and electricity.

NUCLEAR ENERGY:
Radioactive elements like uranium can be used to generate heat, which can be a source of useful energy. Cost, safety, and waste disposal concerns surround nuclear power, making it a controversial energy source.

ENERGY EFFICIENCY IS IMPORTANT, TOO!

When we think about our current energy needs as well as those of future generations, we must think not only about the *supply* of energy, but also about how to reduce our *demand*

for it. We will have to restructure our world—to design our houses, office buildings, factories, and all our vehicles to be *much* more energy efficient. And there are many things we can do right now to be more efficient. We can reduce unnecessary consumption of material things, all of which use energy to produce. We can better insulate our buildings, use less heat in winter and less air conditioning in summer, and ride bicycles or use public transportation instead of driving cars, for example. But we will also need to apply all of our human ingenuity to INVENTING new ways to do things that require less energy.

THERE ARE THINGS WE LEFT OUT, OR GREATLY OVERSIMPLIFIED, IN WRITING THIS BOOK.

Earth is an extraordinary planet, and its complexity is daunting. In our attempt to describe the essence of the fossil fuels story, we have left out, or greatly oversimplified, some very important processes that shape our planet. Here are a few other pieces of the puzzle:

THE OTHER PART OF THE GLOBAL CARBON CYCLE:
Besides what we call the "Cycle of Life," carbon atoms are involved in a very important, but very SLOW, geological cycle that plays a role in regulating the CO_2 concentrations in the atmosphere. When volcanoes erupt, they spew CO_2 into the air. When it rains, some

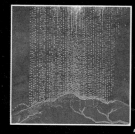

CO_2 is washed out of the atmosphere and, as it flows into the sea, it is involved in a chemical weathering cycle that drives the formation and dissolution of carbon-containing limestone rocks. Unlike the Cycle of Life, it takes millions of years for a carbon atom to move through the geological part of the cycle.

THE EARTH'S INTERIOR:
The Sun is the narrator of our story so we made it all-powerful. This shortchanges the enormous amounts of energy held inside Earth's core. Not only can this "geothermal" energy be captured for use by humans, but it also drives chemical reactions that feed whole ecosystems such

as those near deep-sea volcanoes. The Earth's interior is an integral part of the Earth's energy system. But that is another book!

BACTERIA AND FUNGI:

When we talk of the Cycle of Life and represent living creatures that consume plant life, we have focused on animals, including humans. But

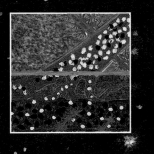

bacteria, fungi, and other microscopic organisms are *of critical importance* in the Cycle of Life, breaking down plant matter that animals and insects have not eaten, and "burning" it as they respire. Collectively, bacteria and fungi consume oxygen and produce CO_2 in vast quantities.

BACTERIA THAT LIVE WITHOUT OXYGEN:

The "last responders" in the global feast on plant biomass are all the bacteria that live *without* oxygen. These "anaerobic" bacteria live wherever they can find a home away from oxygen—including inside our own bodies. Anaerobic bacteria play a *crucial* role in recycling elements required for life on Earth.

SYSTEMS AND FEEDBACK LOOPS:

One of the central features of our planet is that everything—life, water, air, soil, rocks, etc.—is interconnected. It is a system. Systems have feedback loops among their parts: When one part changes, it influences what happens to another, and that influences another, and so on—until the whole system has changed—often in unpredictable ways.

Our planet, with all of its interconnected living and nonliving parts, may be the most complex system imaginable. It took 4.5 billion years to become the place we think of as home. It is constantly changing, and because of the

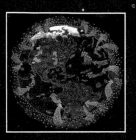

millions of feedback loops its behavior is difficult to predict. Now that humans have discovered and tapped into Earth's energy savings bank—fossil fuels—we have become a dominant force in shaping the planet. We must do all we can to understand the potential consequences of our actions and act accordingly. The future of our species, and that of most others, will be determined by the choices we make.

To our planet Earth
and to those who use your bounty
with wisdom and restraint.

With many thanks, again, to Jim Green!
And to Jake Waldbauer, Roger Summons, Dave Munro, Steve Hackett, Skee Houghton, and Vicki Murphy. Finally to Kathy Westray, Bonnie Verburg, Grace Kendall, and Elaine Markson.

THE BLUE SKY PRESS

For information regarding permission, please write to: Permissions Department, Scholastic Inc.,
557 Broadway, New York, New York 10012.
SCHOLASTIC, THE BLUE SKY PRESS, and associated logos are trademarks and/or registered trademarks of Scholastic Inc.
Library of Congress catalog card number: 2014000215
ISBN 978-0-545-57785-4
10 9 8 7 6 5 4 3 2 1   14 15 16 17 18
Printed in Malaysia   108
This book was printed on paper containing 55% recycled content and 25% post-consumer waste.
First edition, October 2014
Designed by Kathleen Westray

DATE DUE

			PRINTED IN U.S.A.